MYSPACE

M A R K E T I N G

THE PROMOTIONAL REVOLUTION

2nd edition

comedian **business** studio blogger label fashion
game websites club **marketer** photographer station
professional IT journalist television **tshirt** production
artist choreographer magazine **store** candy filmmaker
booking DJ **promoter** instructor **musician**
singer writer **designer** director hair stylist actor agent PR
graphics designer **dating** authors **band** movies res-
taurant **politician** model promoter radio show agency

Nick Jag

MySpace Marketing: The Promotional Revolution

Authored/Published by: Nick Jag
P.O. Box 781764
Orlando, FL 32878-1764
www.nickjag.com

ISBN-10: 1-4196-8034-X
ISBN-13: 978-1-4196-8034-2

Contents

1 Marketing 101   7
     1.1 Goals   9
     1.2 Audience   9
     1.3 Tactics   18

2 The MySpace Network   19

3 Important Basics   21
     3.1 Banner Ads   22
     3.2 Bandwidth   22
     3.3 Phishing   24
     3.4 Copyrights   25
     3.5 Spam   26
     3.6 ID's   28

4 Profile Construction   29
     4.1 Account Choices   29
     4.2 E-mail Addresses   31
     4.3 Display Name and URL   32
     4.4 Style and Image   34
     4.5 HTML Tutorial   36
     4.6 Profile Picture   39
     4.7 Your Story   40
     4.8 SEO   41
     4.9 Top Friends   44
     4.10 Pictures   45
     4.11 Videos   47
     4.12 Statistics   48
     4.13 Downloads and Music   53
     4.14 Newsletter   54
     4.15 Network Channels   55

5 Finding your Target   57
     5.1 General—Demographics   57
     5.2 General—Psychographics   61
     5.3 Music   63
     5.4 Film/Comedy   64

5.5 Profiling   64

6 Promotion Techniques   **67**
   6.1 Invites   71
   6.2 Friend Requests   72
   6.3 Messaging   73
   6.4 Comments   74
   6.5 Bulletins   77
   6.6 Blog   78
   6.7 Forums   81
   6.8 Groups   82
   6.9 Events   83
   6.10 Classifieds   84
   6.11 Videos   84
   6.12 Bots   85
   6.13 Featured   95
   6.14 Top Charts   97
   6.15 B2B   98
   6.16 Banners   99
   6.17 Polls   100
   6.18 Staying Personal   100

7 Additional Promotion Techniques   **103**
   7.1 Whore Trains   103
   7.2 Purchasing Friends   104
   7.3 Purchasing Bulletins   105
   7.4 Purchasing Profiles   105
   7.5 Hit Generators   106

8 Resources   **109**
   8.1 Layouts and Code   109
   8.2 Free Image Hosting   110
   8.3 Free Video Hosting   111
   8.5 Profile Components   112
   8.6 Bots   113
   8.7 Whore Trains   114
   8.8 Purchasing Friends, Bulletins, and Profiles   114
   8.9 Hit Generators   115
   8.10 MySpace Blogs and Forums   115

MARKETING 101

Promotion is becoming entertainment, which not only is cheaper than traditional advertising, but more effective. Through new promotional methods like the MySpace website, you can connect with your audience on a whole new level, yielding more loyal and active customers than almost any other form of promotion. Not only will you be spreading the word about your product or service, but you will obtain fans of your brand. Most companies are eager to get started and develop their brand club, but this "promotional entertainment" is actually one of the final steps in spreading the word about your product or service.

A successful promotional campaign is one that includes research and prep-work in developing the proper methods and correct information that will ultimately produce a beneficial online strategy for your business and help you to measure and maintain your success.

This is what we call marketing

Assuming your product/service has been designed, your marketing campaign will include the elements to successfully launch your product on the MySpace network.

To develop your marketing campaign we need to establish three things:

- **Knowing what you want**
- **Knowing who will give you what you want**
- **Knowing how to get those people to give you what you want**

In lesser terms, knowing your goals, your target audience, and your tactics, which include strategy and promotion will give you a successful marketing campaign. As I mentioned, several businesses—including bands—jump straight into promotional tactics, but understanding your goals and your target audience before-hand will allow you to select the proper tactics when using the MySpace website.

Throughout the book, there will be several examples, links, and codes that are all available on the website,

NickJag.com, listed by chapter. Also on the website are continuous updates on new resources and changing information, along with a mailing list for critical updates of which you should be aware.

Goals (Knowing what you want)

Goals allow you to become organized, keep your eye on the ball, move forward, and measure your progress. Throughout your campaign, you should be setting goals and measuring your results to make sure certain promotional activity is working for you. Doing this allows you to keep track of your progress and discover what is or isn't working for you, and adapt accordingly. For example, a filmmaker might set a modest goal of attaining ten new friends a day on the MySpace website. He may find that an hour a day of "friending" random people doesn't quite meet his expectations, but just commenting on other filmmaker's videos gets him several new friend requests. For each of your promotional activities, you should be thinking, "How can I measure my success?"

Audience (Knowing who will give you what you want)

Knowing who your audience is at all times when promoting is essential to being effective and efficient. It would be silly for a company that manufactures lawn care tools to advertise on a website geared toward a young demographic, but such poor targeting happens every day. There's a good chance you already have an idea of who your potential audience is, or maybe you have done the research and actually know. There's a well-known saying in the marketing world coined by John Wanamaker, father of modern advertising, which goes,

"Fifty percent of your advertising budget is wasted. Problem is, you don't know which fifty!"

The reason so much money is wasted in advertising each year is because an advertisement is the wrong message or directed towards the wrong audience. Either way, advertisers are wasting time and money because they don't understand their audience well enough. Knowing your audience is extremely important to your success, and this is where research comes in. Large companies have very extensive research budgets, constantly redefining their target audience and their positioning. MTV actually hires private researchers to live with teens for a few days and study their habits. Record labels have telemarketing systems that ask people to rate the beginnings of ten or so songs to find what has the most mass appeal. So what do most of these large corporations know that many small businesses don't? It's all about the research!

How do you get started? You should start with market research and obtain everything about the market you are in or plan on going into. Start by researching it on the Internet. Surf industry websites, read blogs, subscribe to RSS feeds. Find trade publications, magazines, and articles at your local library. Check out what your competitors are doing and who they are targeting. If you're a band, this would mean going to concerts of other bands that have a similar sound. If it's a direct product you're selling, you can call your competitor and ask them questions as a student for a research project. You could also talk to their customers in person if they have a storefront location. Be creative!

Throughout your research you should begin to get a better idea of who your target audience is. Once you're confident about who your target audience is, you should research them directly to get specific details. With the information that you obtain from your research you should compile a target customer profile so you can better understand them and keep track of their habits.

On the following page is a blank profile with questions to guide you in your research and constructing a target customer profile. Knowing the answers to these questions is essential to your success.

Target Customer Profile

What is the age range of my customer?

....

....

....

Specific gender?

....

....

....

How does my customer spend their time? What do they like to do?

....

....

....

Where is my customer located?

....

....

....

What appeal does my product/service have to my customer?

....

....

....

What kind of disposable income does my customer have?

....

....

....

What is the average education level of my customer?

....

....

....

Will my customer buy my product/service online, in stores, or both?

....

....

....

What are some of the influences on my customer?

....

....

....

After you have set up a detailed customer profile of your target audience, you can begin to research them directly in reference to your actual product or service. Your research should somehow connect your target audience to your product/service. There are three main ways to research them - surveys, interviews, and online stalking.

The easiest and most common way is to start with your friends, family, and coworkers. This network can be somewhat effective as long as the people you research are close to your target audience. Your grandfather probably has different taste in music than teenagers.

Surveys

Surveys work well for simple and short questions. Here are some tips in making your surveys:

- Keep your survey under 10 questions
- Provide answers for your user to choose from
- Do not to use loaded questions (e.g. Isn't my music awesome?)
- Do not ask for contact information

An easy way to send out surveys is to create a free online survey using Zoomerang **(https://signup. zoomerang.com)**. After constructing your free survey, you can e-mail your survey's URL to your target audience. Users can fill out the survey online and you can view the cost-free results for up to 10 days with easy-to-read answer graphs as shown below.

1. Which do you prefer?			
Rock		5	36%
Rap		3	21%
Country		1	7%
Pop		4	29%
Other		1	7%
	Total	14	100%

Interviews

Having interviews with your target audience can provide you with extremely informative answers to your questions and ideas and additional information you didn't even think of. The downside, of course, is that interviews are typically more expensive than surveys and take much more time.

To make the best use of your time, conduct group interviews if applicable or schedule single interviews one after the other. To cut down on costs, advertise interviews on free websites, such as Craigslist.com, Facebook.com, or MySpace.com. You can also use the newspaper classifieds. Depending on your target audience, twenty to thirty dollars per hour is about right for compensation. Also, include refreshments as this helps to make your guests more comfortable in opening up and sharing information.

Online Stalking

I titled this research method "Online Stalking" because, ironically enough, many people would consider some of the following techniques in obtaining their public information to be very "stalkerish" if they were per individual basis.

For our means, to "stalk" your target audience online is to find and learn anything you need to know about them and answer many of your questions with the information they've provided you. Because there are many different types of information you might need to collect from your target audience, I will only introduce you to the techniques of finding and gathering information.

First and foremost, you must find a sample of your target audience to research. Facebook and MySpace are some of the easiest places to start since there are so many details about a person. Using the advanced search applications for either website, find ten or so active users and create a file for each user for which you can log information, trends, etc. Active users will have a recent login date, a good flow of comments, and a good amount of information available on their profile.

A key area to find good research information is in a user's blog. Many times it may be easier to just search for users who write or have written about a subject that you are researching. For example, say I need to research what type of pizza users like better, Domino's or Papa John's. MySpace, Live Journal (**www.livejournal.com**), and Digg (**www.digg.com**) are great places to find information like this and any additional information you might have never thought of. The way I would go about searching for this is to use one of the following Google queries:

dominos papa johns site:livejournal.com
dominos papa johns site: blog.myspace.com
dominos papa johns site:digg.com

Using the "**site:**insertwebsitehere.com" search method
of Google can be extremely helpful in finding detailed
information. Unfortunately, little information will
show for the Facebook website since the network is
currently private.

To find additional information about one of your key
users, you can search on their primary user name.
Many people go by the same user name, usually the
first part of their e-mail address, when signing up to
different websites. Simply just querying this user name
in Google may turn up a plethora of information
about your user and websites he/she is signed up to.
Sometimes it may be useful to work backwards with
the user name. For example, if you have obtained a user
name from a private blog, you could search for the user
name within the MySpace website. You could even
append popular e-mail domains (i.e. aol.com, hotmail.
com, gmail.com) to the user name and search for the
user on Facebook by e-mail address.

In addition to establishing "who will give you what
you want," your research should also provide you
with a greater understanding of the brand image
or personality you should portray throughout your
promotion.

Your brand image is extremely important and is
controlled by packaging and promotion, and has little
to do with your actual product. For example, Steve

Wilhite, COO of Hyundai Motors, is struggling to reposition Hyundai as a premium brand that competes with Lexus or BMW. Although Hyundai is rated #3 in initial quality by J.D. Power and Associates, their cheap brand image has made their improved product quality no match for the established premium image of high-end car manufacturers.

In an environment such as the MySpace site, a brand image is especially important to develop associations with the adolescent users in their search for identity. Before you begin promoting, you need to know what your brand image will be and why that image will work for your company. To get a general idea, look at your competitors and their brand "personalities." Don't copy them, but learn from their styles and improve on them.

Tactics
(Knowing how to get those people to give you what you want)

Every business has a strategy or several strategies that it uses to reach its primary goal (typically to make money). Throughout the rest of the book you will be introduced to several marketing methods and resources from which you should construct your strategies. You will most likely be refining your strategies as you measure your success. Overall, having a basic understanding of all the tools that are available to you will aid in developing successful strategies and an overall successful marketing campaign.

THE MYSPACE NETWORK

The MySpace website began in 2003 and is, of course,
the most popular of all the social networking sites.
The average MySpace user is male or female with
an age ranging from 16 to 34. Users typically spend
their time making new friends, customizing their
own profile, discovering new music, watching videos,
and writing about their day. Commercial profiles are
generally represented by bands, comedians, filmmakers,
dating sites, clothing companies, record labels, authors,
studios, television shows, box office hits, and even
politicians!

Why has the MySpace website grown so rapidly?
One of the main reasons the site has received so
much success is due to what so many users ironically
complain about—clutter. Combine the hard-to-find

information with complete personal customization options, add a few million bands and entertainers to the mix, and you have yourself a social network where people spend hours just browsing around.

As a marketer, you will be using the MySpace website as a social network for your brand, and not a direct spam vehicle. Several businesses randomly spam users relentlessly, and users hate it! Not only do these methods not work, they're against the website's Terms of Service (TOS). MySpace administrators have become strict and very efficient in removing such unnecessary spam content. Building a network of dedicated fans of your brand with the setup and promotion techniques I discuss will allow you to properly build your brand and increase your revenue using the MySpace website.

IMPORTANT BASICS

These important MySpace basics should enlighten
you on the precautions you need to take and terms you
should understand before you begin your marketing.
The MySpace TOS (Terms of Service) document
is constantly changing, and I encourage you to sign
up to the NickJag.com mailing list to receive critical
information about important updates and ongoing
changes.

The MySpace service is not intended for businesses
other than bands, comedians, or filmmakers, but
you can still have a successful profile like hundreds
of thousands of existing businesses. Applying the
methods of this book will help you to operate a stable
and successful profile without fear of losing your hard
work or getting in trouble.

Banner Ads

The MySpace website is a free service that is funded by advertising. Each profile on the site has a banner advertisement at the top. Some businesses and users remove this advertisement to enhance the look of their profile. Many bands use header graphics that sit on top of the advertisement, blocking it from view. Removing or blocking the advertisement is against the MySpace TOS and can result in the swift deletion of your account. Plain and simple, don't remove it.

Bandwidth

Every word, picture, song, video, or other form of media on the internet is located on a computer at some location. When you connect to, or request, a website, your computer is essentially connecting to that other computer and downloading those files. Your MySpace profile works the same way in that most of your media will be located on a MySpace server, and when a user goes to your profile, they download the media onto their computer. MySpace profiles have a type of automatic bandwidth allocation that increases as needed.

Bandwidth is like the front door to your website. If your door is only big enough to let ten people in at once and, suddenly, 1000 people want in simultaneously, entry for each person will be a slow process. Gradually increasing the traffic to your profile will allow your door to grow steadily with your traffic. The way to do this is a steadily-paced promotion campaign. If you're running a large advertising or promotion campaign that you know will generate a lot of traffic, be careful. If you're profile is not ready to handle so many users at once, your profile won't be accessible to everyone, and you will lose potential customers and fans. Obviously cutting down on the amount of media you put on your MySpace profile will improve its ability to adapt to large audience sizes.

Here are some guidelines to follow when embedding media into your profile:

- Make sure no two medias automatically play at the same time.
- Make sure your background image is less than 50 kilobytes. To check this, view the background image properties.
- Never upload a large image and use HTML code to resize your image, always resize the image itself first and then upload it. An excellent, free program to resize pictures is the Photo Resizer (**www.rw-designer.com/picture-resize**).
- Don't post an excessive amount of images on your profile page. Instead, organize your information in folders and/or galleries and link to it. You can also use a slide show.

Phishing

A recent popular scare on the MySpace website has been the use of fake password phishing profiles. These profiles and/or websites are made to look like the MySpace homepage that prompts the user for their login information to proceed with the last action. A user then enters his or her username and password, unwittingly submitting it to illegal spammers. Most successful attacks are done by automation and spawn nearly 100,000 username and password combinations each time. Popular celebrities, bands, and businesses alike are often the target of such attacks because of their extensive networking abilities. Celebrities such as Lindsay Lohan and Paris Hilton have been the victims of such phishing attacks, and as a business, you need to protect yourself.

When logging into the MySpace website, always manually type **www.myspace.com** in your browser. If you should ever be prompted with an additional login screen, manually type in **www.myspace.com** again to safely return to the MySpace homepage.

You should also be weary of MySpace resource websites that ask for your MySpace username and password. There are thousands of resource sites and only a handful of them are very reputable companies. Putting your login details in the wrong hands could put your account details in black market phishing lists where many spammers could take over your account and spam your network and friends. With so much time and effort put into your profile and network, it's best not to risk sending your information to these websites unless you know you can trust them.

Copyrights

Copyrights are a fairly simple concept, yet very misunderstood. Here is some basic information about copyrights:

- Any work (graphic, drawing, recording, etc.) that is in tangible form is automatically copyrighted. Registering your copyright with the United States Copyright Office offers you further protection, but it is not always necessary.
- Copying any works that you do not own without permission is infringement, even if it is not for commercial purposes. The author may seek legal remedy against you for your actions.
- Making compilations (background graphics, a musical remix, etc.) from others' works without their permission is also copyright infringement. The author may seek legal remedy against you for your actions.

Please note, the above information should not be taken as legal advice. If you need legal advice, consult an attorney.

Copyright infringement has become a big problem for the MySpace corporation. Many users construct fake music profiles and upload popular bands' music to these profiles, therefore allowing them to add the music to their own personal profile and even offer the song for download through the profile.

In response to this problem, MySpace has hired the California-based company Gracenote to help find and block such content as well as implementing a digital fingerprinting technology called "Take Down Stay Down" to keep copyrighted material from being re-uploaded.

When you upload your media content, make sure you have the copyright permission to do so. When uploading your material, the MySpace website will log your IP address and possibly certain characteristics of your profile. If you are caught uploading copyrighted material for which you do not have the rights, MySpace administrators will delete your account and ban you from using their services. It is also possible you could face charges through an IP trace and "John Doe" lawsuit, similar to what the RIAA uses in its lawsuits against music piracy.

Spam

Promotion has been important in the development of the MySpace community, but massive amounts of spam are detrimental to it. Not only does spam hassle the users of the service, but it costs the company millions of dollars each year.

Brand building and promotion are very different from spamming. Professional spammers send out thousands of untargeted messages each day soliciting a variety of different online websites and/or products. These professional spammers are what the MySpace website targets in its efforts to clean the site of unwanted mail, but that doesn't mean your business couldn't get in trouble, either.

Many businesses, including bands, tend to over-promote their products or services and run the risk of getting their account deleted or even sued in some cases (we'll talk more about that later). Although basic promotion techniques such as messaging are essential to spreading the word, focusing on the individual customer and using a combination of techniques will return stronger results without risking your profile or your company.

The quality of your audience is much more important than the quantity. Throughout the promotion techniques discussed in the book you will learn the limits that you should apply to your activity so you don't run into problems. You will also learn how to back up your profile and your friends should you run into a problem.

ID's

Every profile on the MySpace website has an ID number that is generated by ascending order at the time the member registers. The ID number is located in the URL of a MySpace profile.

http://profile.myspace.com/index.cfm?fuseaction=user.viewprofile&friendid=**12345678**

These ID numbers will come in handy for tracking your marketing efforts as you will discover later on.

PROFILE CONSTRUCTION

Account Choices

The first thing you must decide before you sign-up to the MySpace site is what type of account you will register with. There are four different types:

- Comedian
- Filmmaker
- Music
- Standard

Each type of account has different content available as well as different networking opportunities. Here's the breakdown of each different account type along with my suggestions.

Comedian & Filmmaker

If you're a comedian or filmmaker, these accounts are obviously for you. Both the filmmaker and comedian accounts have a front video list that displays movie information and statistics, making it easy for users to browse and view your work. You can also choose to feature a list of screenings (if you're a filmmaker) or gigs (if you're a comedian). These are particularly useful and easy to update when you're traveling. Besides comedians and filmmakers, any business that needs a continuous array of videos and possibly schedule information should consider using one of these accounts. Such businesses could include a television show, online-mini series, documentaries, etc.

Music

Music accounts allow you to stream music and add a show schedule to your profile. Obviously, these accounts are designed for bands, but music-related companies often find these profiles to be useful in their features and networking opportunities. Music producers, recording studios, compilation records, and record labels are just some of the businesses that often use a music account.

Standard Member

Standard member accounts may not seem like anything special, but almost all of the features included with the above accounts, excluding an updatable schedule, are available to a standard member. If your business is not directly related to music, film, or comedy, I suggest using a standard account because of their versatility.

E-mail Addresses

When you sign up for an account, you will need an e-mail address. Whatever e-mail address you decide to use, do not change it. Unconfirmed reports suggest that MySpace administrators flag accounts with changed e-mail addresses. Why would they do that? If a malicious user has taken over an account, they will usually change the e-mail address.

If you are getting a new e-mail address for the purpose of this account, I would suggest a Gmail **(www.gmail. com)** address (Google E-mail). Here's why:

- Over 6 gigabytes of space (you'll most likely never run out... ever... ever... ever)
- Fast searching - find anything by keywords, e-mail address, etc. in seconds.
- Extensive foldering and labeling options - great for keeping your e-mail organized and you efficient.
- A very effective spam filter
- An automatic address book and auto-completion of e-mail addresses by name or e-mail.

I've used every popular online e-mail client and can tell you from experience, Gmail is the best, hands down. If you plan on using a Gmail account with your MySpace account, I recommend setting up Labels and Filters in your Gmail account for the MySpace automatic notification e-mails. This way, any MySpace e-mails (new friend requests, messages, etc.) will go directly into your folder of choice and leave the inbox for more important e-mails.

Display Name and URL

After you sign up for your account, you will be asked a series of questions. You can skip most of them or change your choices later if you like. The two most important pieces of information are your display name and your URL. The display name is extremely important because it carries the most weight for searching and is the title of your profile. It is listed under "basic info" in the "edit profile" section. The display name should be the exact name of your business. If you're a band, don't abbreviate your band name. If you do need to use two names for some reason, I suggest registering another account and putting a link to your primary account. Links and other codes are listed later in the chapter and are available on the website, NickJag.com.

Your MySpace URL is the address at which your profile will be located, and unless you have a music account, the URL name you choose cannot be changed. Here's an example:

http://www.myspace.com/**mybusinessname**

You should keep the URL name the same as the display name, but without spaces. When people are searching for your business on Google or Yahoo!, having your business name in the URL helps your profile to show up at the top of the results. After you have created your URL name and title, you need to submit your MySpace profile to search engines.

You should manually submit your site to these search engines:

Google: www.google.com/addurl
Yahoo!:   search.yahoo.com/info/submit.html
MSN: submitit.bcentral.com/msnsubmit.htm

The URL you submit will look exactly like the example shown previously, with **yourbusinessname** appended to the end of **http://www.myspace.com/**. It will most likely be weeks or months before your profile is actually indexed by the search engines, which is why it is important to get an early start. It is usually of little value to submit your URL to most other search engines, because they typically feed off the results of the three listed.

If you haven't picked your actual business or band name yet, I would suggest keeping it simple, short, easy to remember, and most importantly, unique. There should be no other business or band with that name. Once you have an idea, search the name in quotes on Google and see what comes up. If there are a lot of results (thousands), you might want to change the name.

Style and Image

Most people aren't designers, and MySpace profiles are more often than not a bit rough on the eyes. Creating the correct image for your audience is one of the keys to your success online. This can be easily achieved by taking a look at what style your competition or similar businesses are portraying. A profile for a travel agency will obviously differ in style from a metal band. Once you're able to find your image, you can style your profile using profile coding knowledge, a pre-made profile layout, or a profile layout generator. Searching in Google for "MySpace Layouts" or "MySpace layout generator" will return thousands of results.

A great way to really stand out from your competition is to create a customized layout that doesn't conform to the MySpace structure. These custom structured profiles are called *div layouts*, which are similar to the custom profiles for sponsored business spots that run in the tens of thousands of dollars through the MySpace advertising department. To create your own custom-structured profile or div layout, there are a few free websites that offer generators, pre-made layouts, and the code on how to do one if you're up for the challenge. Having these one-of-a-kind profiles can be very beneficial for businesses that are trying to really stand out (bands especially), but for businesses that are trying to stay low and keep a small business image, a regular styled profile will probably work better. Either way, there is a list of resources at the end of this book and on the website, NickJag.com, which I find to be the best to use. Make sure when editing your profile that you do not delete the banner advertisement or the "block user" link on the contact table.

When filling your profile with content, you will be confronted with a choice of where to put certain information. Over time, the standard MySpace layout has created an established, intuitive profile structure for users. Follow this established, intuitive diagram below to design for maximum effectiveness in delivering your content.

Main Picture(s)	Media, News/ Blog, Schedule
Contact Menu (message, add)	General Info, Story, Soft Sell
Secondary Media (downloads)	Secondary Media (videos or pics)
Company Details	Top Friends and Comments

To keep your profile looking good, you should disable HTML in your comments. Several spammers often post comments with large images that take users' attention away from your profile. Disabling HTML in your comments section makes sure spammers won't get the best of your account. To do this, go to "Account Settings" on your profile home. Click the "Change Settings" link for "Profile Settings," and check "Disable HTML Profile Comments."

HTML Tutorial

When editing your MySpace profile, you'll need to know some of the basic HTML tags and code. Here are the most popular and useful tags, also available on the site, NickJag.com.

Paragraph Tags

To separate your text and sections into paragraphs, we use the paragraph tags:

```
<p>Put the paragraph here</p>
```

Break Tags

Break tags allow you to move to very next line:

```
If you put a break at the end of this sentence...<br />
You can write on the very next line...<br />
Or the next line
```

Bold

To make text bold you can use this simple tag:

```
<b>This text is bold</b>
```

Italics

To use italics:

```
<i>This text will be in italics</i>
```

Links

To create a hyperlink to Google:

```
<a href="http://www.google.com"> Link Title </a>
```

If you would like to have the link open a new window when the link is clicked on, use this code:

```
<a href="http://www.google.com" target="_blank">
Link Title </a>
```

Images

To insert a picture:

```
<img src="http://www.mypictureurl.com/mypic.gif">
```

Now lets combine the link and image codes together.

Picture Links
To link a picture and "Click Me" to Google:

<a href="http://www.google.com"><img src="http://www.mypictureurl.com/mypic.gif">
Click Me </a>

Headings
To use different heading sizes:

<h1>Heading Size 1</h1>

This becomes...

Heading Size 1

<h2>Heading Size 2</h2>

This becomes...
Heading Size 2

<h3>Heading Size 3</h3>

This becomes...
Heading Size 3

Horizontal Rule
To add a horizontal line use:

<hr />

Combining Tags

Make sure to open and close tags in the correct order:

This text is bold and italicized

In using hex color codes with more advanced HTML, make sure not to include the "#" in front of the color code. The MySpace website does not allow this character, most likely for security purposes in encoded ASCII text.

Profile Picture

Your profile picture is like your calling card on the MySpace site. It needs to draw people in, stimulate recognition, and ultimately get them to click through to your profile. Several people use photos, but I suggest using a professional logo or drawing because people can typically remember that better than a photo, and it also stands out the most. A professional profile picture is one done by a professional! Make sure you get a graphic artist or someone that knows what they're doing to create your image.

A recent popular trend is animating the profile picture, drawing more attention to the profile. This works well, especially if you have an announcement to make, such as an upcoming CD release date. Any professional graphic artist can do this, just make sure it's optimized for the web in terms of file and image size. Also, make sure that your profile picture is consistent with your brand image and not too commercial looking.

A couple years ago, spammers ingeniously developed fake, attractive female profiles with attractive profile pictures. For a while, these profile pictures brought in a great deal of traffic.; however, millions of fake profiles later (presently), using a photo of any attractive person as your profile picture will most likely label your profile as spam and could decrease your potential traffic, not to mention present ethical problems for your business.

Your Story

In the music business, one of the most important things for a band to have is a story. The same is true for any business with a MySpace profile. Stories not only help make your business more interesting, but are the backbone of brand building. Specifically, the content in your profile should all be based around a story instead of a sales pitch. Take a small sunglass shop in California as an example. Let's say their customers have been telling them how hard their store is to find. Instead of relocating their shop, they could turn this issue into a marketing campaign. To do this, they create a MySpace profile for people who have successfully found their store—an "I found the Taylor Sunglass Shop" MySpace profile. It could be themed with a treasure hunt style and focused on the

difficulty of finding the shop. This challenge would
actually appeal to people and stimulate an interest
in discovering the shop. Successful customers would
become proud and loyal fans of the brand, instantly
wanting to become their MySpace friend as if it was
their trophy.

There are many businesses with successful profiles that
have great stories, some of which I have posted on the
website, NickJag.com. Because the MySpace service
typically frowns upon commercial profiles, however, I
won't list any specific examples here in the interest of
protecting the businesses.

When developing a story for your business you should
think about your business' strengths and weaknesses.
Keep your target customer in mind at all times and
consider selling points that he or she may be interested
in to incorporate within your story.

SEO

SEO stands for search engine optimization. Whether
you have a website or not, it's important that your
business' MySpace profile is indexed well in the major
search engines. Earlier we discussed how to get your
website submitted to the search engines, but now you
will optimize your profile to increase your chances of
being at the top of the search results. To start, you must
research and define the keywords that people are using

to find businesses like yours. The Overture Keyword Selector (**http://inventory.overture.com**) is a great tool to help you discover what search terms are most popular and have the most volume.

Once you have a list of the popular keywords being used to find your business, you need to use those keywords throughout your profile. Embed the keywords in a heading, text paragraphs, and image tags. Image tags are text descriptions that are visible when a user's cursor hovers over your image. Images and tags are discussed in the Pictures section.

Another SEO technique is to use the keyword(s) or keyword phrase(s) you would like to be searched for as text that links to your MySpace profile. This is called obtaining backlinks. For example, let's say you have a MySpace profile setup for your real estate company that sells houses in Houston, Texas. Using our Overture Keyword tool from above, here are some results that I've obtained when searching on "houston real estate:"

Searches done in January 2007	
Count	Search Term
129921	houston texas real estate
19780	houston real estate
1312	houston heights real estate
1282	houston tx real estate

When looking at the results, I can see that the query "houston texas real estate" is far more popular than my original criteria, "houston real estate." Sometimes less popular and more detailed keywords, usually called "long-tail keywords," can be much easier to rank for in search engines. Therefore, I could also choose to rank and optimize for "houston tx real estate" instead. Ultimately, your choice of keywords and/or phrase depends on the competition for the keywords. Generally speaking, any phrase that obtains over 1000 monthly searches will have considerable competition, and therefore will be less feasible for your MySpace profile to rank for.

Once you've chosen your keyword phrase, you should start obtaining backlinks to your profile with your keyword phrase inside a hyperlink. Recall from the HTML tutorial section that a hyperlink looks like this:

```
<a href="http://www.google.com"> Link Title </a>
```

After replacing the google.com URL with your MySpace URL, replace the "Link Title" with your keyword phrase. Here is an example of a backlink that applies to our Houston Texas Real Estate profile:

```
<a href="http://www.myspace.com/
myrealestateprofile"> houston tx real estate </a>
```

Having your backlink(s) on sites related to your content, in this case, real estate, can help your backlinks provide stronger positioning power in search results.

Here are some ways to start obtaining backlinks:

- Post on popular and relevant forums with your backlink in your signature.
- Post contributory comments on relevant blogs with your name and backlink at the bottom.
- Post comments to relevant articles on large social networking websites, such as Digg.com or Slashdot.com, with your backlink.

Beware of spamming your backlink, as this will get you deleted and your IP address marked as spam on most communities. Make sure your postings are well thought-out and contributory to a topic. Over time, your links will accumulate and start bringing in targeted traffic from search engines. Remember that relevant link building is a slow process and seeing your profile in search engine results can take several weeks or months.

Top Friends

What was once known as the "Top 8" is now your "Top Friends." As you collect friends, you can edit your top friends to display your best or favorite friends on your profile. You can choose to display anywhere from four to forty top friends (in multiples of four), and you can edit your top friends by clicking on the "Change my Top Friends" link below your initial top 8 friends on your profile home.

Many businesses will choose to do contests for a Top Friends spot, which would encourage you to open more available spots; however, I recommend keeping it at eight and making sure there are no attractive profile pictures in your Top 8 so visitors have less incentive to leave your profile.

Pictures

The MySpace site allows users to upload an unlimited amount of pictures with the ability to organize them into albums and provide captions. Alexa.com reports that the photo pages on the MySpace site get more traffic than the actual profile pages; with this in mind, I suggest you take full advantage of the photo albums by posting a variety of pictures that supplement your story and interest viewers.

To display your images on your profile's front page, you can use a slideshow or HTML code. The MySpace site has an easy-to-use slideshow that can display your photos. This tool is located under "Add/Edit Photos," and I recommend using the "Random" style. Several other photo services are listed under the Resources chapter in this book.

The other way to display a single photo on your profile's front page is to use HTML code. After you have uploaded your photo to the MySpace site or other picture hosting service, view the individual photo you would like to post to your profile. If you're using Internet Explorer, you should right-click on the photo and select "Properties." You will see the URL for the photo. You must highlight and copy this URL as shown below.

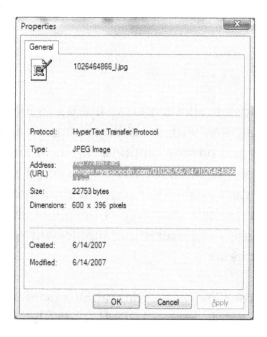

If you are using Mozilla Firefox, right click on the image and select "Copy Image Location."

Once you have your image path (URL) copied, you should paste it in the following code...

```
<img src="PasteImagePathHere" alt="Image Tag Here">
```

In addition to pasting your image's path, you should add a description or your SEO keywords as an image tag. Your finished code should look similar to this, except your image path will be very different, and much longer than this one:

```
<img src="http://www.myspace.com/584_l.jpg" alt=
"Description or Keywords">
```

Now that you have your image code, you should paste it in the "edit profile" section where you would like your image to display. If you need additional assistance, there are many HTML tutorials listed under the Resources chapter and on the website at NickJag.com.

Videos

When uploading your videos to the MySpace site, there are a few things you will want to remember. First, make sure the title is accurate and appealing. Also, make sure you include relevant tags that are keyword heavy. Having good tags will help your video to appear when people are searching through the videos. Separate each keyword with a comma, and do not use phrases. Remember to think of synonyms and alternative spellings for your keywords also. Keep all your settings public so your videos have the best chance of being displayed. Finally, select three categories for your video to increase your chances of being found.

To embed a video in your profile and/or other content, scroll down below the video to find the "Video Code." Copy and paste this code in the content editor where you would like the video to show up. The YouTube website has a similar "Embed" code that you may use to insert YouTube videos within your MySpace content. When embedding YouTube videos, make sure to click the "customize" link to the right of the code and select "Don't include related videos."

Statistics

Statistics are extremely important information for any business, band or otherwise, in helping to assess the effectiveness of your promotion efforts. The basics of measuring start with counting the visitors to your profile.

MySpace has a built-in counter that features your total profile views on your profile home. For media profiles (bands, comedians, etc.), the number of plays and/ or downloads are shown in their respective players. Logging this information before and after your promotion efforts (messaging, commenting, bulletins, etc.) can be very helpful in assessing how effective your campaign was.

For example, you may find that, on average, while

sending out 200 messages returns approximately
100 profile views, writing 200 comments may return
almost 300 profile views, or vice-versa (depending
on your target audience and message). Knowing this
information will help you to make the most of your
time and efforts when promoting.

In addition to using the MySpace built-in counter,
there are several external counters (usually in the form
of images) that can be placed on your profile to count
how many users have visited your profile. HitsLog
(**www.hitslog.com**) provides a very useful counter
for MySpace profiles that allows one to see an array
of information about a visitor. Another very easy one
to use is the Free Myspace Profile Counter (**www.
freemyspaceprofilecounter.com**).

A helpful, but risky alternative to counters are trackers.
Trackers log users that visit your profile and display
their information (including profile link) to you when
you log into the tracker site. MySpace administrators
have become very strict on the use of these, blocking
several of the popular trackers and warning users
against installing them. Many of these trackers will use
your account to spam others or take over your account
all together. Given the risk involved, I would advise
against their use and sticking to counters.

Another great technique in gathering statistics is using
website redirects. This particular method is a little more

advanced and takes some extra time to setup, but can yield a great deal of useful information.

A redirect is simply a webpage that redirects to another webpage. In this case, you or your website developer would create one or more webpages that automatically redirect to other pages, probably your MySpace profile, or parts of it. After the page(s) are created, some type of statistics program should be installed. I recommend using Google Analytics because of the advanced information it provides about your visitors. Once your page(s) have some type of tracking method installed, they may be hyperlinked to for whatever purposes.

Here is an example:

1. A rock band sends out several comments and messages about an upcoming local concert with a link to more information about the concert. (MySpace provides bands with a little section for their concert details)
2. The links in the comments and messages go to separate webpages on the band's personal website, but redirect the user back to MySpace (and the concert information) so quickly that the user would never know they left MySpace.
3. The rock band can then check their statistics and see which redirect page got more hits - the page in the comment link or the page in the message link, there by ultimately revealing

which promotion method was more effective -
comments or messages.

4. If Google Analytics was installed, the rock
band could also see, on a map, where the users
were located (below). More advanced filters and
tunnels can also be setup with Google Analytics
to measure conversion ratios of certain
promotion methods (messaging, commenting,
etc.) returning or completing defined goals (CD
purchases, downloads, website hits, etc.).

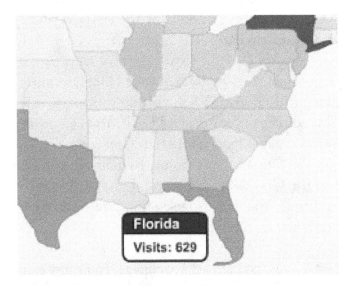

Above: Google Analytics visitor map sample image

To begin using the redirect method, you can construct
your webpages with Google Page Creator (**http://
pages.google.com**). In constructing your pages, select
the "Micro Ghost" template by clicking the "Change

Look" link in the top right-hand corner. To setup your simple redirect, click "edit html" in the bottom right-hand corner and insert the following code:

```
<meta http-equiv="Refresh" content="0; url=http://
www.yourwebsitehere.com">
```

Replace the "http://www.yourwebsitehere.com" with the URL you would like to redirect to (in our example this was the concert details on our MySpace profile). To find the URL you would like to redirect to, navigate to the desired webpage and copy the URL in your browser's address bar.

You can finish creating or save your Google webpage by clicking "Publish." When visiting your page, it should redirect to your desired URL. You can create many more pages by clicking the "Create a new page..." link on the Site Manager home. Remember, you don't have to use Google Page Creator, I just used that for this example. You can also use other free webpage creators such as Yahoo!, Geocities, or Angelfire.

After you have created your webpage, you must setup some type of statistics program with it for it to be useful. As I mentioned, I recommend signing up to Google Analytics **(http://google.com/analytics)**. In signing up, you must add your website domain. If you are using Google Pages, this would be:
yourusername.google.com

After submitting your domain, Google will give you a special code to place in your webpages. You should place this code above the redirect code in all of your pages. Once the code is in place for each page, press the Publish button again to save each page.

Unfortunately, Google Analytics code cannot be used directly on MySpace profiles because the MySpace website prohibits the use of JavaScript coding.

Downloads and Music

Offering downloads on your profile is a great way to remind your users and customers about your brand. Here are just some of the files you could offer:

- Desktop Wallpapers
- AOL Instant Messenger Buddy Icons
- Screensavers
- E-Posters
- Business Trading Tips
- Music
- Videos
- Pictures

If you're a band, offering your media for download can be a good or bad thing. On one hand, offering downloadable media can prevent a user from going to your profile again, but on the other, it can produce dedicated fans by launching your media to the top of their brand ladder and their everyday entertainment. In the professional world, big artists will only offer a one or two minute clip of their music on their MySpace Music Player to be streamed and possibly downloaded. This helps users to become attracted to the artist's music, but still preserves the need to buy the content since users cannot listen to an entire track.

In addition to making music downloadable, artists can allow users to add the artists' songs to their profiles. This is by far one of the best marketing techniques offered by the MySpace site of which an artist can take advantage. When friends and users add your song to their profile, viewers of their profile will hear your music and can easily add your song to their profile too, becoming a sort of exponential promotional movement. This option is available under the song manager settings and should be taken full advantage of by offering incentives to friends or users for adding the artist's music to their own profiles.

Another MySpace feature artists will find useful is the Snocap MyStore (**www.snocap.com**). This is an online digital music store that is placed right on your profile.

Newsletter

Having a newsletter list where users of your profile can sign up to is a great way to keep in touch with your audience as well as promote your products and/or

services. Many businesses find it useful to re-brand the
newsletter into something more appealing, such as a
VIP or Club sign up where users receive special offers,
freebies, or top secret information. Be careful about
putting a newsletter form directly on your profile.
MySpace administrators have increased the security of
the site, which displays an alarming warning message
when users submit information to another website
from a MySpace profile.

*"Warning: You are submitting information to an outside
site. This could be an attempt to steal your username and
password."*

This warning message could make your users think
you're trying to trick them into giving you their
password. Instead of posting a form on your profile
directly, you should link to an external form where
users can sign up to your newsletter. Having a
webmaster is particularly useful in this instance, but
there are a number of low-priced websites that offer
online newsletter services.

Network Channels

If you have a standard account (non-music, non-film,
non-comedian), you can make use of the network
channels. In the "edit profile" section, there is a link
called "Networking" which allows you select three
networking affiliations for your profile. Networking

affiliations are searchable under the "Search" link on the main navigation bar and are used quite often for people or even businesses looking for a specific business type in their area.

Finding Your Target

The built-in MySpace searching techniques are a marketer's dream. Knowing of and how to use these techniques will allow you to find and target your customer down to the smallest details.

Quick Tip: When searching a website for a known text string, use the browser search tool under Edit ▶ Find on this Page, or the keyboard shortcut Ctrl+F. Make it habit to use this tool, as it will drastically improve your internet browsing efficiency.

General—Demographics

To search MySpace profiles by demographics, you can browse user profiles using the tool under the "Browse" link on the top navigation bar. When in the

Browse section, click the advanced tab on the right-hand side of the "Set Browse Criteria" box to display your complete searching options. This browsing tool is the most popular and most used searching tool for marketers using the MySpace site.

The following criteria are available in your searching options:

- Gender
- Age
- Social networking purpose
- Marital status
- Location by ZIP code
- Photos
- Ethnicity
- Body type
- Height
- Smoker
- Drinker
- Sexual orientation
- Education
- Religion
- Income
- Children

Keep in mind that many users choose to skip some of the questions above, which could exclude a large portion of your target audience from your result set if you're searching on too many details. To remain effective, you should start out by searching on a small set of criteria and increase it if the size of your result set is too large and/or broad. Orientation, religion, and income are typically the most unset profile details.

You may order your results in a way that you find useful by:

- Recently updated
- Last login
- New to MySpace
- Distance (from a ZIP code)

To minimize abandoned profiles or fake users in your result set, you should make sure both boxes are checked under the photos criteria and sort your results by "Last Login," located at the bottom of the "Set Browse Criteria" box.

Another very useful searching tool is the Classmate Finder under the "Search" link (right next to Browse). This tool is great for event marketing because of the pre-existing viral networks set up in the school. Searching by school also allows you to keep track of your efforts better by grouping. The LiveJournal school list can also help you find schools that meet your target profile **(www.livejournal.com/schools)**.

After you find schools you're interested in targeting, searching on the MySpace network for the school will give you a list of all the students that have or are attending the school. You can then narrow your search results by a number of demographic and school-related criteria.

One of the other, lesser used search tools is the "Find a Friend" tool under the Search link. The purpose of this tool is to find a single person you may know, but combining this tool with the Baby Name Wizard Name Voyager tool can produce a very powerful search technique (**www.babynamewizard.com**).

The Name Voyager tool allows you to see popularity statistics for baby names. For example, entering "Britney" into the query produces a graph that increases drastically throughout the 1980s and 1990s, peaks around 2002, and has since declined. You can use this tool to build a list of names that correspond to your target's age, gender, and ethnicity characteristics, criteria that a user might have falsified or not set at all. After building your list of names, you can search each name using the "Find a Friend" tool and narrow your results down by ZIP code.

The Classmate Finder and Find a Friend tools are particularly useful in their ability to be saved in your favorites unlike the Browse tool. Once saved in your favorites, you can mark your promotion efforts and pick up right where you left off.

To search for people that are 16 and 17 years old, you

must change your birthday under the "Basic Info" link on the "edit profile" section so that you are under 18. You must then log out and log back in for the changes to take effect.

To search for people that are 14 and 15 years old, you must change your age as described above and then tag a middle school or high school to your profile under the "Schools" link on the "edit profile" section. Make sure you select "In Progress" as your degree type or your school might not show up. After you have tagged a school, you should log out and log back in for your changes to take effect. On your profile home (not your profile), you will notice a link to your new school. Clicking this link will take you to the school's page where you may "View All Current Students."

Make sure you use a separate profile when changing your age, since changing your age in your actual brand profile could limit your features or searching optimization. More information on using multiple profiles is discussed later in the Promotion chapter.

General—Psychographics

Psychographics are attributes of a person's interests or lifestyle. Finding all the people who like Jimi Hendrix would be an example of targeting by psychographics. In addition to searching the entire MySpace network, you can also choose from the drop-down menu to search the following areas of users' profiles:

- Blogs
- General interest
- Music interest
- Movies interest
- Books interest

To search by psychographics, you should use the "MySpace Search" box located under the Search link on the navigation bar. It is set to search all MySpace profiles by default. This comprehensive search can be useful, but you may find it easier to search the individual interest sections or users' blogs to obtain more quality results. The following are a few examples of search techniques for different businesses and products.

To find potential subscribers for a new teen magazine:
      Search: Books Interest ▶
          Keywords: Seventeen, Teen People

To find potential buyers of an iPod case for hikers:
      Search: General Interest ▶
          Keywords: iPod, Hiking

To find new fans for a rising swing band:
      Search: Music Interest ▶
          Keywords: Swing, Benny Goodman

Another search tool for Psychographics is the
"Affiliation for Networking" search tool under the
Search link. This tool allows you to search users who
are networked in a specific area such as fashion, radio,
or photography, as well as defining a specific sub-field,
role, and keywords. For example, if I were part of a
band targeting booking managers for a tour, I would
search:

> Music ▸ Administrative ▸ Booking

Or if I were targeting ballet dance instructors:

> Dance ▸ Education ▸ Instructor ▸ keyword:
Ballet

Performing a search on the latter search criteria yields
567 results, for which you can then narrow down your
psychographic search by gender, age, and/or ZIP code.
It's obvious how powerful and useful this networking
tool can be for targeting any type of audience.

Music

To search a complete listing of bands, click on the
"Search" link in the MySpace Music section (that's
under the "Music" navigation link). Use the "Set Search
criteria" box on the right-hand side to narrow your
results.

For our purposes, useful music searches include:

- Genre
- Band Name/Influences/Sounds Like
- Location/City/ZIP Code

And you may choose to sort your results by:

- Plays
- Friends
- New
- Alphabetical

Whether you're looking for new startup bands in Florida or established bands in Alaska, you should have no problem finding your audience with this tool.

Film/Comedy

Searching for filmmakers or comedians is just like searching for bands. Click on the "Film" or "Comedy" link on the main navigation bar. Next, click the "Filmmaker Search" or "Comedian Search" link. On the right-hand side will be the search tool to narrow down your results.

Profiling

Another easy way to find your audience is to find a profile whose friends make up your target audience.

This is particularly useful for bands that have a similar sound to another band. Choosing small or medium sized bands will generally yield better results since their fans have a more intimate and dedicated relationship with the bands. Mentioning the band or profile you found the user from and relating it to your own profile is a great connection point. You will see later how bots can automate the task of gathering these profile ID's for you.

PROMOTION TECHNIQUES

In an effort to curtail spam, MySpace administrators have placed daily limits for a user's actions on the site. Different actions can sometimes add up to different amounts, but the idea is that any comment, message, friend request, event invitation, post, etc. is counted as one action. The usual limit is 400 actions a day (a day meaning 24 hours from the last action), but just because this is the limit doesn't mean you should push it. Typically, a profile account will be deleted within a few weeks or less for just 300 actions a day; however, it is by no means an exact science. The site purposely mixes up the limits so spammers have a difficult time knowing how many actions in a day they can get away with. Having an older account helps to increase your stability, but there's nothing set in stone when it comes to promoting.

So how do you market to more of your target audience without risking your profile and account? The simple answer is to have more profiles. While this is against the MySpace TOS, many promoters have been using additional accounts to comment or message users with a link to their legitimate profile, minimizing the chances of having their legitimate profile deleted. Many MySpace promoters are also using additional profiles as a series of legitimate profiles. The benefit of having numerous legitimate brand profiles is the friends' perception of a more intimate relationship with a smaller profile and being able to target multiple demographics with a slightly different message. The only precaution multiple profile owners have had to take before was ensuring that the content wasn't duplicated in any way, including the title or the URL, which MySpace administrators are able to track.

Now, however, account deletion is now becoming the least of a business' worries. The MySpace legal department has begun suing many businesses that send out bulk messages or comments, and the line between promotion and spam is beginning to blur.

TheGlobe, a company who promoted their VoIP service through such methods, was sued for having 95 profiles and sending out almost 400,000 messages. The MySpace Corporation settled out of court with TheGlobe for $2.55 million. Although this promotion activity might be considered extraordinary to some, there are hundreds of existing businesses that maintain or even exceed this promotion level on the site today.

The question now becomes: how do you promote your business without getting deleted or sued? Simple—use your profile, not your actions (messaging, comments, etc.), for promotion. To stay safe, your actual promotion should be mixed into your profile content and your actions should be used for connecting and networking, not promoting. There are a number of ways to do this that are explained throughout this chapter.

If you're a band, filmmaker, or comedian, you most likely don't have to worry about getting sued for heavy promotion, as this would be a disaster for the MySpace PR department. In fact, the site even expects such promotion, as evidenced by the option to block group and event invitations from such entertainers. And although I wouldn't recommend most businesses to use multiple profile promotion techniques, bands, filmmakers, and comedians can usually get away with it. To use the technique you simply post a link to your actual profile inside the message from your promoting profile.

A precaution that every business (band or otherwise) should take is to refrain from multi-linking to any affiliated commercial websites (especially affiliate programs or other spam-related content) in their messages, comments, or profiles.

The MySpace site has been rerouting, tracking, and grouping outgoing links in these areas through a website called MSPLinks **(www.msplinks.com)**. Any link that is manually submitted in these areas is rerouted to the MSPLinks website with the original URL encoded and appended to "msplinks.com." When clicked on, the converted link quickly reroutes the user to the desired page. For Example:

When an outgoing link to **http://www.google.com** is submitted in a comment, message, or even a profile, the resulting link will be **http://www.msplinks.com/ MDFodHRwOi8vd3d3Lmdvb2dsZS5jb20=** This link will still take the user to the Google website, but can now be logged and tracked by MySpace.

Links that constantly appear on the MySpace site are flagged as possible spam along with the profiles they appear on. If your business relies on many (thousands of) commercial links, you should post the address as text and not a link. This way the URL is not tracked, and the user can copy and paste the URL in his or her address bar.

It should be noted that links don't always have to be entirely commercial for them to be marked as spam through the MSPlinks system. If a band sends out an extreme amount of messages with a link back to their profile promoting their upcoming free album, they could still be deleted for abusing the messaging system and sending out too many messages. Generally speaking, MySpace administrators only go after companies that are spamming their commercial links all over the site, but they have been known to take down bands that abuse the messaging system.

To sum up all of this complicated information:

- An action is a comment, message, or friend request.
- When first starting out, do not go over 50 actions in a day. You may gradually increase your actions to 300 a day over a few weeks, but never exceed 300 actions in a day.
- If you are using more than one profile to send out messages with links, make sure you don't send out too many (over one thousand in one day is excessive). If you need to send more, write your URL as plain text, not as a link.
- It's best to advertise your services lightly on your profile and not in messages, comments, etc.

Invites

Sending out MySpace invitations is a feature that is underused, but can be very powerful. If you have an established mailing list for your business, or even just close friends, finding existing contacts and sending out invitations can bring you the most loyal MySpace friends that will keep activity up on your profile. High activity on your profile page will keep other users interested in your profile. Few things are worse for your brand image than having two comments on your profile, three months apart.

To start, you should first import your e-mail contacts into MySpace. You can do this by loading e-mail addresses into a Gmail, AOL, or Yahoo! address book. After uploading one of these service's address books, the MySpace website will compare your list of e-mail addresses with the e-mail addresses of existing users and automatically send your matches friend requests. This is by far one of the easiest ways to get friends on the MySpace site. If you have more addresses than can fit into one of the e-mail program's address books, you can upload a portion of your e-mail addresses into a service's address book, upload the address book to MySpace, and repeat again and again until you have run out of addresses.

After sending existing matches friend requests, the MySpace site will send the remaining e-mail addresses an invitation to join MySpace and become your friend. About a week later be sure to make use of the built-in reminder feature to track and remind anyone who has not responded to your request.

Friend Requests

Once you've pulled in all the friends and customers you have from the outside, it's time to start finding friends on the inside. Friend Requests used to be one of the better actions for promotion because a receiver could easily check your profile and add you as a friend. Now, however, MySpace has implemented a large "Mark as spam" button with every request. If enough users click that button, and they will even if you're a band, your profile gets marked as spam and is deleted.

To prevent deletion, friend requests must be sent out in small amounts (less than 50 daily) to extremely targeted users. The idea here is to keep a large percentage of your friend requests being accepted, which will decrease your overall chances of being marked as spam. One way to do this is to send additional friend requests to bands. Bands will almost always accept your friend requests, especially large bands. These constant friend accepts should offset any users marking your requests as spam.

Messaging

Messaging is one of the easiest and fastest ways to get the word out about your business. The advantage of messaging is that you don't have to be a person's friend to send them a message. Any MySpace promoter knows this, which is why messages are the most used form of promotion on the site. A typical MySpace user will see at least one message a day from someone promoting their business, usually a band. To deal with this problem, there are now links to block the user, delete from friends, flag as spam, and report abuse. If you receive too many blocks or flags, your account will be deleted.

To get around this issue, many bands and businesses use a couple fake profiles to send out messages. This works well because the risk of deletion does not extend to a band or business' main profile. When registering new profiles for the purposes of promoting, keep in mind that MySpace is probably more lenient with a band profile promoting than with a standard profile.

When sending your messages, make sure that the subject and message are personal and have appeal; otherwise it might not get read. Also, offering some type of incentive or giving the user something to do helps in making messages more effective. A really simple trick in constructing effective messages is to ask a non-open-ended question in every message.

Comments

Comments are messages that can only be left by a user's friend and are displayed on the user's profile. The benefit of comments is that anyone who can view the user's profile can view your comment, giving your comment far more reach than a message. The problem with commercial comments is this: not only might your friend delete your comment for trying to promote to his or her friends, but he or she may block you, ultimately increasing your chances of being marked as spam and deleted from the MySpace website.

To utilize the comment system effectively, you should post personal, all-text messages that have little to do with your business. This will ensure you keep your friend and your comment up. Friends of your friend will be more inclined to visit your profile when your comment is not commercialized. Many businesses seem to never understand this simple concept—people don't like advertising. Your soft sell should be on your profile, not on other people's profiles, and especially not in the form of a huge banner on other people's profiles. Nothing tells your friend you could care less about them than a foot long banner about your upcoming CD release or five comments in a row to stand out better.

Wrong way to comment:

DON'T MISS SAMSON KINGS CD EP RELEASE THIS FALL!!!!! ITS THE BEST MUSIC EVER!!!!!!!!!!!!!!!!!!!!!!!!!!!!!!!!

Right way to comment:

Hey, it's Samson. I noticed you're a big fan of Tenacious D—so am I! I don't know if you've ever been to one of their shows or not, but they seriously rock. Anyhow, glad

*you enjoy my music, and let me know if
you have any comments or suggestions. I'm
releasing my CD this fall with some of
the songs on my profile. If you have a few
minutes, let me know what you think and
maybe what order you think the songs should
go in. Thanks!*

Notice how, not only do we make the comment
personal, but we establish an objective for the fan—to
order the songs on the profile. This simple task could
drive a lot of traffic and a longer stay to the profile.
Make sure when you're posting your comment that
it's not too long or short—about 4 to 6 sentences is
perfect. This way it stands out from the rest of the
comments, but not enough to look out of place.

Instead of posting images or links in your comments,
you should be posting more comments. Building this
public relationship with your friends through comment
conversations will draw trusting eyes to your profile.
If your friend Jacob and you talk through comments
often, Jacob's friends will not only be going to your
profile to see who you are, but will also trust you since
Jacob does.

Another use for commenting has been promoting on
very popular profiles and videos. Since these areas get
thousands of views every hour, posting a comment here
can get you a lot of extra traffic.

Bulletins

Bulletins allow you to message all your friends at
once. Each friend has a list of the bulletin headlines
on his or her profile home that their friends have
recently posted. The problem with bulletins is that
they get pushed down by the bulletins of other friends.
Obviously, if your friend only has 25 friends, your
bulletin could be up there for a few days before it's
pushed down. However, if one of your friends has 400
friends, your bulletin will probably not be seen unless
you post it when he or she is online. For this reason,
it's critical that you post your bulletin at the peak hours
of usage so you have maximum effectiveness with your
bulletin. Generally, traffic is highest during prime
time, but the peak hours for your audience may vary
depending on their location and other demographics.
Through experience with your audience you will begin
to better understand at what time your bulletins are
most effective. To help you get started, below is a chart
of when to post your bulletin depending on the time
zone you're in.

Pacific	Mountain	Central	Eastern
6:00pm	7:00pm	8:00pm	9:00pm

What many businesses do is post several bulletins
throughout the week. Most friends won't seem to mind
this since they won't even notice all your bulletins, but
it's best to change the headline and message a bit so

they don't all look the same for the people that will see all your bulletins.

When posting your bulletins, the headline is very important. Use personal headlines, as they have most success. Also, make sure you post bulletins or a series of bulletins for important events only. Posting irrelevant bulletins will leave you as the profile who cried wolf. The fewer bulletins you post, the more interested people will be when you do post.

Blog

A blog is a diary/news/announcements section where you post articles and users can read and comment on them. Blogs have become very popular within the past few years and can really help you connect with your audience. To manage your blog, there is a "Manage Blog" link on your profile home.

It may sound obvious, but your blogs should be rich in content and interesting to your readers. Many businesses will repeat the story over and over again, and many times it's a promotion gimmick! Not only should you not repeat content in your blogs, but keep the majority of your blogs free from promotion. Try writing content that keeps your readers interested and coming back like a hilarious YouTube video or an important news event that your readers could relate to. If you can, embed the content, such as a news story

or a video so you keep your readers on your profile
and not surfing the rest of the web. After your readers
appreciate your content, many of them will subscribe
to your blog. Subscriptions to your blog will notify the
subscribers for when you post a new blog, driving more
traffic to your profile.

Another way to obtain subscribers is through your RSS
feed. An RSS feed is a kind of text file that updates
itself with headlines of a news or blog source. A user
can enter an RSS feed URL into services such as
Yahoo! Alerts or Live Bookmarks, and when the source
releases new content such as a new blog post, the
subscribed user can receive a message with the headline
of the content. Messages can be received a number of
different ways, including e-mail, instant message, or
even by text message. Teaching your friends about RSS
feeds and encouraging them to receive announcements
about your blog can really help to drive traffic and
build trust in the products/services you offer.

Where can you find the content to post that will
interest your readers? Depending on your market and
what audience you're targeting, you would benefit
most by finding other professional blogs that produce
the content about which you can post. Try using the
Google Blog Search to get started (**http://blogsearch.
google.com**).

Once you've got your blog going, you should join a

blog group to which your content applies. A blog group is just what it sounds like—a group of blogs. There are no real benefits for a blog creator so it's best to join groups that are established and very popular. To sort a list of blog groups by popularity, find a category that applies to your content and click the "Total Member" link on the right-hand side. Join groups that have several members so your blog gets a better chance of being seen.

To spice up your blog a little, you can change the styling of it under the "Customize Blog" link in the blog manager. Customizing your blog can be useful in establishing a special image associated with your rich content.

Another suggestion when posting your blogs is to switch between three different privacy settings:

- Public
- Friends
- Preferred list

Setting your privacy to public will allow everyone to view your blog and comment on it. This is nice, because it allows everyone the chance to read your content, but you also need a type of club that will draw in friends. Titling an interesting topic as "For your eyes only" or something mysterious that only friends can view can actually increase your friend requests since many will be curious to read it. Just make sure there is some interesting content with which to follow through. Friends are great, but to really establish a special connection and brand spirit, you should use the preferred list privacy setting once and a while to encourage people to request to be on your preferred list so they can read the remainder of your secret blogs. To add people to your preferred list just click the "My Preferred List" link in the blog manager. You could also use the preferred list privilege as an award for contests or points in street team assignments.

I mentioned anyone can view your comments when they are set to public, which is the standard and most used privacy setting. When a blog is set to public, viewers can also comment on it (recall only friends of a profile can comment on the main profile). This commenting ability can be a promotion tool in itself. Finding popular profiles that have a similar target audience to yours and commenting on their blogs is another great way to drive traffic to your profile. Since blog readers obviously like reading, majority of them will read your comment, so make it good!

Forums

Forums are places where users can post messages, reply, and interact with each other. Under the Forum link on the main navigation bar, there are a number of forums with thousands of threads in each. You can post your own thread in a forum or respond to others'. You will most likely get a negative response if you try to promote your business in the forums unless you're a band, for which case there's a promotion section for each genre. Although the main forums won't yield much traffic from promoting, businesses can still benefit by responding to other people's posts and contributing to a conversation. This can bring a good amount of traffic, just be sure to contribute to posts your target audience is reading.

In addition to a directory of students, each school profile also has a forum where students talk about events or classes quite often. Any businesses that host events could make great use of these school forums by promoting their upcoming local event. To access a school profile, use the "Schools" tool on your profile home to the right-hand side below the "Cool New Videos" and the "Featured Profile." Also note that there is an event section under the classifieds on the school profile for which you may also post events.

Groups

A great way to get all your friends talking and build your network is to create your own group. The groups section is located under the "Groups" link on the main navigation bar. Each group has its very own forum where your friends and outside users can interact under your name. Once again, the privacy issue is at

your discretion, but I recommend making your group
public since users are very likely to join a group they're
interested in. Make sure when you choose the group
URL that it's similar to your profile URL, and don't
forget to post the link on your profile and talk about it.
Once you've created your group, you can invite all your
friends to join.

Some groups can get very big, much bigger than the
administrator's profile. For example, the BodyBuilding.
com group has over 100,000 members, but the
BodyBuilding.com profile has less than 500. To
communicate with all of the members of the group,
each group has the ability to send out its own bulletins.
Take advantage of this bulletin tool to keep group
members involved and interested in the group. Make
sure you disable the ability for members to send out
bulletins through the group or you will have a bunch of
spam being sent to all your members.

Events

Creating and promoting your event is really easy on
the MySpace site. Whether you're a band, club, or a
traveling trade workshop, promoting your event can
raise awareness about your brand and bring in the
customers. To promote your event, click the "Create
New Event" link under the "Events" link on the main
navigation bar. Use a picture in the "Long Description"
section by inserting html to make your event look more

interesting. When creating the event, you'll be able to invite your friends via a message as you would when creating a group. Once posted, encourage attendees to spread the word by clicking "Blog this" or "Bulletin this" on the event page.

Classifieds

Most businesses should find the classifieds section to be of great use. On the right-hand side of the navigation bar, there is a link to the "Classifieds," which allows you to post or respond to classified listings in a number of different categories. Particular categories that businesses may find useful are any sub-categories of Services or MySpace Friends. Make sure you remember to flip through the cities at the top when you're posting or promoting.

Videos

Videos are one of the easiest and most effective promotion techniques on the MySpace site. Anywhere you're posting content (profile, blogs, groups, etc.) you should try and incorporate a relevant video.

Three things videos do better than any other media:

1) Keep people on your profile longer
2) Help people remember your profile better
3) Generate word of mouth promotion

A really great use for videos is video-blogging. Video blogs have a great impact on users and a higher rate of penetration than a normal text blog. People have more patience for videos and are more likely to watch a video about what you have to say rather than read about it. If you need assistance in developing your own videos, there are plenty of resources on the website at NickJag. com to help you along.

For maximum effectiveness, use MySpace videos when uploading your own content and YouTube videos for other people's content. This allows your personal videos to rank better and for users to comment easier while the YouTube videos keep visitors' eyes on your profile.

Bots

Bots are programs that automate the functions of the MySpace site. They can be your best friend or your worst enemy. Of course, the TOS strictly prohibit using bots, but most of the automated systems have gotten pretty good at disguising themselves, becoming virtually indistinguishable from real users. To counter this, MySpace administrators have gone after many of the bot owners, successfully in most cases, but there are still many that exist.

Over time, one bot company has lasted longer than any other, still issues updates, and still provides customer support - FBP (**www.nickjag.com/friendblasterpro**).

Since this bot is the most trusted and widely used bot for MySpace promotion, I will go over its features, how to use it appropriately, and what to expect.

The bot includes seven different actions:

- Gathering ID's
- Sending Messages
- Sending Comments
- Sending Bulletins
- Sending Event or Group Invites
- Sending Friend Requests
- Accepting Friend Requests

Gathering ID's

Gathering profile ID's is the most important operation of the bot. This allows the bot to compile a list of everyone you want to message, comment, or send a friend request to. This operation also allows you to save your own friends.

To save your own friends, go to your profile, select "Gather ID's from All Pages" and press Start. After the program is finished gathering your friends' profile ID's, click the "Save List as..." button directly above the list. If, in the future, should you need to message all your friends, you can click the "Import from file..." button and import your friends' profile ID's. You may find it of great assistance to open the tutorial (under Help) to view more details about the different operations as we proceed.

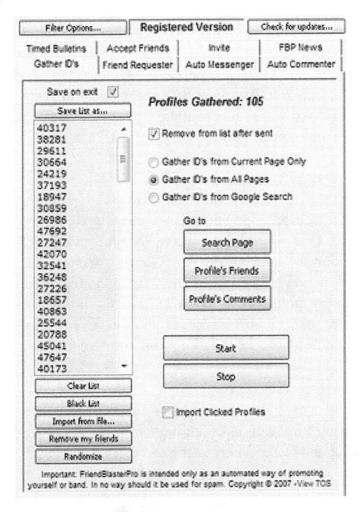

Before you begin gathering profile ID's for the purposes of promoting, be sure to set your "Filter Options" near the top. This will allow the program to target the users you are gathering. Also, depending on how you want to setup your lists, you might want to select "Remove from list after sent."When you're ready, locate a profile for which you would like to gather the friends of, select "Gather ID's from All Pages," and press "Start."This will compile a list of targeted users' ID's to the left. After you have gathered a sufficient amount, click the "Randomize" button near the bottom left-hand corner. Randomizing these ID's will help to shadow the bot from MySpace.

Another very useful operation is the "Gather ID's from Google Search" operation. This operation allows you to search for specific keywords on MySpace profiles after clicking the start button. Any Google operator will work here. For example, typing "i'm a photographer" with the quotes yields over 700 MySpace profiles. If I were selling a new camera or photo software, that would be an excellent list of profiles to target.

Sending Messages

Having a bot can make sending out messages much easier and faster. Many of the messages will require you to enter a CAPTCHA code as shown below:

CAPTCHA filters are distorted images of letters and/

or numbers that you are required to type and submit to continue an operation.

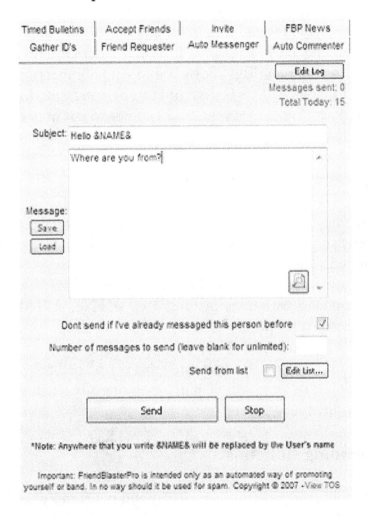

When sending out messages, make sure the "Don't send if I've already messaged this person before" option is selected. Also, you can include a person's name in the message or subject by using the text **&NAME&** as shown in the picture on the previous page. If you have many accounts that you send messages out from, you may find it useful to multi-chain these accounts by adding and selecting the accounts under Options > Multi Chaining. This allows you to send out messages over many accounts instead of just one, increasing the number of messages you could safely send out in one day.

Sending Comments

Sending out comments is just like sending messages, only you are restricted to your profile's friends. The added advantage a bot brings is the automated ability to switch back and forth between HTML (comments with links, pictures, etc.) and Non-HTML comments for profiles that do and do not allow HTML comments. Also, making sure the "Don't send if I've already commented this person before" option is selected will help in preventing any repeated commenting.

Sending Bulletins

Sending out bulletins is very easy and much more effective with a bot. A bot can post your bulletin multiple times at a specified time interval and delete any previous instances of it, making it look like a fresh bulletin each time and ensuring you don't flood the bulletin boards. Make sure the Anti-flood option is checked and do not close the program or it won't be able to post your bulletins.

Gather ID's	Friend Requester	Auto Messenger	Auto Commenter
Timed Bulletins	Accept Friends	Invite	FBP News

Bulletins sent: 0/0

Auto post 100 times once every 240 minutes

Anti-flood ☑

Send from list ☐ [Edit List...]

Subject: This is my bulletin

Message:

    It will repeat every 240 minutes for 100 times deleting
    each previous time before posting the next.

[Send]

Since the bot deletes each previous post before it posts a new one, you don't have to worry about posting too often since most users will never catch on. In the previous picture, I setup my bot to post every 240 minutes (4 hours) for 100 times. This will take approximately 17 days to complete. Obviously, I wouldn't let it go this long since my message would probably change before then, but you can see how these numbers are used.

Sending Event or Group Invites

After going to a group or event's main page, you can specify which of your friends you would like to invite by narrowing on location, friend ID's, or your entire list ("Friend Lists"). The bot can cycle through and invite your friends much faster than any human could. With this in mind, creating and promoting an event could actually replace messaging or commenting your friends when you need to get a message out fast. For example, creating an event such as "Our new music is out," posting details on the event page with a link back to the music, and using the bot to invite each and every one of your friends is an easy way to tell several people about something quickly. The targeting by location option could prove very useful if you post an event for each of your tour dates.

Sending Friend Requests

Sending out friend requests with a bot is extremely easy and you usually won't run into any CAPTCHA filters until about 50 or so friend requests. Remember to use caution when sending out requests, making sure your gathered ID's are extremely targeted since users are able to very easily click the "Mark as spam" button.

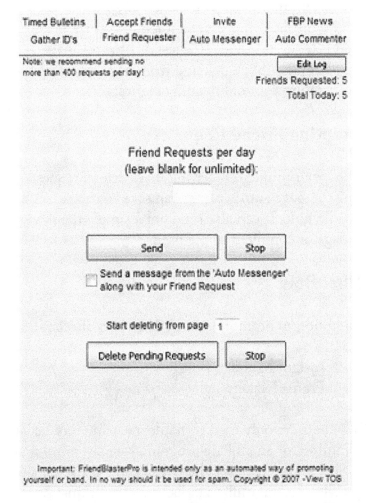

To add bands as we discussed before, gather profile ID's from the Music Directory pages (Music >

Directory). Many bands are fake or abandoned and might not answer your requests. These "pending requests" can and should be deleted with the bot's "Delete Pending Requests" button. If you have new requests, locate the page on which any old requests start on by observing your sent requests (Home > Friend Requests > Sent Requests). Type this page number in the "Start deleting from page" input box to start deleting your old pending requests.

Accepting Friend Requests

When your profile is receiving many friend requests, using the bot's auto accepter can save you some valuable time. It can also send out a simple thank you message or comment to the user.

Other Bots

In addition to promotion bots, these bots also exist:

- Instant Message Bots
- Profile Makers

These bots are only used by hardcore spammers, usually promoting for an affiliate program. Keep in mind that MySpace administrators hate these bots the most and have filed several million dollar lawsuits against people who use them. Using these bots is completely out of the scope of marketing and would be considered spam.

Featured

Almost every section of the MySpace website (Music, Videos, Filmmakers, etc.) has a featured section where sponsored or non-sponsored profiles are featured and get thousands of views a day. There are four ways to get featured:

- You ask for your profile to be considered
- You know or get to know a MySpace employee who puts in a word
- MySpace employees stumble upon your profile and want to feature it
- Pay up!

Requesting your profile to be featured is rather easy. Depending on what type of profile or media you would like considered, follow the instructions below. All e-mail and website addresses are available on the website, NickJag.com. If an address has changed, it will be updated on the website also.

Bands

Use the following form to request a music profile to be featured:

```
http://collect.MySpace.com/index.cfm?fuseaction=misc.
contactInput&primarySubject=5&secondarySubject=21
```

Videos

Send a message and the link of the video to:

videos@myspace.com

Comedian

Send a message and a link to the profile to:

http://www.myspace.com/APlaceForComedy

Other

Send a message and the link of the profile to be featured to:

http://collect.MySpace.com/index.cfm?fuseaction=misc.
contactInput

The success rate of requesting your profile to be featured is pretty low due to the number of submissions. To increase your chances as an artist or comedian, your profile should be very established with scheduled tour dates and quality music and/or videos before you make your requests.

Of course, knowing MySpace employees has its perks, but if you're like most, you probably don't know anyone who works there. No problem! Finding employees of MySpace is really not that hard. One of the easiest

ways is to pull up Google and search on the following
query:

"I work at MySpace"

Don't forget the quotes. This will bring up over 27,000
sites of people claiming to be MySpace employees. Just
remember to establish a relationship with an employee
first before you start promoting to him or her.

The Myspace site claims that most of their featured
profiles are found by employees working diligently
to find the best, funniest, most different, and most
entertaining material on the site. While this may be
true for the most part, paying your way in is always
accepted. This cross between advertising and public
relations has become a standard expense in many major
corporations' promotion budgets. The cost of launching
a sponsored profile generally depends on the time
frame for which it is promoted, but is usually in the
tens of thousands of dollars.

Top Charts

The MySpace site has top charts for artists, filmmakers,
comedians, and videos. These charts not only bring
in additional traffic, but are a continuous source to
many entertainment scouts. The video and filmmaker
charts are produced by a single video's "Top Plays."
For these charts, choosing categories or genres that

are non-competitive, such as the Westerns genre for filmmakers, can land you an easy spot in the top ten. Not only might you get a few extra visitors from it, but it would make an excellent image-boosting topic for your next blog.

The artist and comedian charts are calculated by a secret ratio of "Today's Plays," total plays, total views, and possibly friends, with the most emphasis on "Today's Plays."

Many artists have been using special programs and/ or code to synthetically enhance their views and plays, which is discussed in more detail under Hit Generators. To take advantage of the charts without being dishonest, bands and comedians should make one of their three genres a non-competitive genre so they have a higher possibility of ranking in the top ten for that genre.

B2B

B2B stands for business-to-business, as in doing business with another business. There are several other businesses on the MySpace site, many of which are always seeking partners, promotion material, and even entries for contests and publicity. This is especially true for bands. There are hundreds of magazines, websites, studios, and other music-related businesses that want you to submit your profile to them.

One way of finding these businesses is with Google. Search on queries such as:

"to be featured" site:MySpace.com

"our giveaway" site:MySpace.com

"top 8 contest" site:MySpace.com

vote "Battle of the Bands" site:MySpace.com

Don't forget the quotes. Searching on these queries will return hundreds of profiles that are most likely having some type of competition, contest, or submission to be featured in some way. To view the saved version of a website with your keywords highlighted, select the "Cached" link as shown below.

MySpace
Meet people from your area in the country and keep in touch. Includes groups, games and events.
www.myspace.com/ - 48k - Jun 16, 2007 - Cached - Similar pages

Banners

A popular promotion tool on the MySpace site is the banner. A banner is a graphic for your business that your friends can put on their profile. When a user clicks on the banner, they are directed to your profile. A typical banner size is 475×70 pixels. It's best to have a professional graphic designer spend 30 minutes to

make your business a nice banner, but Google is full
of websites that offer custom banners—just search on
"MySpace banner maker."

Polls

Getting users to interact with your profile is an
excellent way to build brand loyalty and keep them
coming back. One easy tool you can use is a poll. There
used to be several MySpace poll makers that allowed
you to put the poll directly on your profile page, but
since the site has increased their security, the daunting
warning box pops up if you're submitting information
to another website, as mentioned in the Construction
chapter. Fortunately, you can use poll creators that
create an external webpage for your poll that you can
link to from your profile. One such poll maker can be
found at **www.yourfreepoll.com**.

Staying Personal

Throughout all your promotional efforts, there's one
thing to keep in mind—you're dealing with people. The
better you make people feel about themselves and the
more you connect with them, the more they will trust
and like you.

The most successful businesses on the MySpace
network are the ones with a small amount of friends
that are very attached to them. It may sound cheesy,

but just using the upcoming birthdays list on your profile home to send out birthday wishes to your friends can earn a lot of trust and connection.

Remember to always follow-up with people and keep conversations going. Bands in particular have a bad reputation of not responding to friends' comments and messages. The more personal you can be, the better. The mentality/strategy of "big and hard-to-get" does not work here. A great way to better connect with your audience is to maintain a LiveJournal and post the link on your MySpace profile **(www.livejournal.com).**

ADDITIONAL
PROMOTION TECHNIQUES

Whore Trains

Whore trains are a list of users' profiles that want more friends. You can join the train (list) to have people "whore" you as a friend or you can "whore" the people on the train.

The problem with whore trains is that they're filled with spam profiles, the only users that want thousands of untargeted friends. Most spam profiles appear as legitimate people, sometimes even holding conversations between themselves using an integrated network of fake profiles. Ironically enough, what results from whore trains are thousands of spam profiles spamming each other.

With the massive increase of spammers in the past couple years on the MySpace site, whore trains have entered into a new market—advertising. Most whore trains now include the ability to purchase front spots, ensuring you whore yourself most effectively. So how effective are the whore trains? Based on a representative sampling of whore trains in early 2007, approximately 80 percent of the whore train users are spammers and 15 percent are bands. Almost any profile that uses the whore trains to gain friends will find their comment area plastered with various spam and promotion.

For most businesses, whore trains just won't work. Most legitimate MySpace users despise whore trains and do not want friends that use them. You want your friends to feel special and to trust you. Having thousands of fake friends will only give you a bad image and additional, unwanted sales pitches. The best thing to do if you need more friends is to add bands. Although bands will still comment and message every so often, they aren't half as bad as whore train friends.

Purchasing Friends

There are plenty of services out there that claim to add thousands of friends to your profile for a price. The majority of these services add whore train friends to your profile, not legitimate targeted users. Even if they do offer targeted users, it's just a numbers game to them. To market your business successfully, you need to be interested in the quality of friends, not the quantity.

Purchasing Bulletins

Purchasing promotion bulletins that are sent out through popular profiles is a common practice in the MySpace business world. There are usually options to target the bulletin to a specific demographic, but take caution since most accounts that are selling bulletins have fake, whore-trained friends. Most businesses will find bulletin buys to be quick traffic generators, but not necessarily useful for retaining visitors. Depending on your business model and what profile is sending out the bulletins, you may find purchasing bulletins to be very effective. The going rate is about five to ten dollars for a bulletin promoted to 25,000 friends. At this price, most businesses can afford to try the technique at least a couple times. When writing your bulletin, remember that the headline is very important. Headlines have the critical role of grabbing a user's attention—a task best accomplished with personal headlines.

Purchasing Profiles

A popular trend in 2006 was to sell or purchase established MySpace profiles—that is, profiles with thousands of friends. A business could then continuously spam their new friends until the profile was deleted or until they had no more friends.

MySpace administrators have since started to crack down on this, and it has become more difficult to buy or sell profiles. As a business, these established profiles may seem like nice opportunities, but they're not. Just like buying any other MySpace service, most of the friends these profiles have are untargeted and/or whore train friends. Another problem with purchasing a profile is the unknown history of the account. If the account was used for spamming, you could find yourself in a whole mess of trouble. If you're seriously considering purchasing an account that claims "real friends," randomly sample some of the friends to see if they're legitimate. It's getting harder and harder to tell fake from real, but a good indicator is how many pictures they have. A real profile almost always has at least 10 unprofessional pictures.

Hit Generators

Hit generators are programs or services that you can purchase to generate a certain type of traffic such as profile views, music plays, or movie plays.

For businesses other than bands, comedians, or filmmakers, generators are practically useless. Most businesses need to stay below the radar since commercial profiles are technically not allowed on the MySpace site, but there is a potential increase in image for bands, etc. to have more views or plays. Many artists use these generators to increase their chances of being in the top ten for a daily chart. The problem with using these generators is that MySpace administrators have certain ways of tracking such usage and might disable certain features of the offending account or even delete it altogether.

It might be possible to avoid the detection of inflating of your profile views by spreading the actions of a generator over a long period of time, but it is more difficult to increase music or video plays and get away with it. To increase music plays, most generators simply reuse the code for your music player to increase the plays, which is against the MySpace TOS. This is basically the same tactic as putting your music player into bulletins or in friends' profiles so your player gets more plays. Although some bands have gotten away with reposting their music players, many have also been deleted. Most likely, the bands that succeed in reposting their music players without compromising their account do so by reposting the music player in other accounts in such a way so that their main account is not tied to nor has any influence in the reposting. If you're interested in learning how to repost your music player, check out the tutorial at NickJag.com.

RESOURCES

This chapter includes the links to many products and services that have been discussed throughout the book. I encourage you to check the website, NickJag.com, for additional links and updates.

Layouts and Code

ProfileHTML
This website offers excellent HTML and CSS tutorials and examples for beginners or people who don't want to remember all the tags.
www.profilehtml.com

Customyzer
An easy to use MySpace layout editor.
www.customyzer.com

Create Blog
Many high quality div overlay and custom profile layouts to give your business or band a distinctive look. www.createblog.com

Rubbur Layouts
An attractive and professional div layout generator that can take any profile above and beyond. www.rubburlayouts.com

BBZ Space
A div overlay generator for experienced HTML and CSS users. www.bbzspace.com/overlay

Squidoo
An excellent div overlay tutorial for steps on how to create your own entirely custom MySpace profile. http://www.squidoo.com/myspace_div_overlay/

Free Image Hosting

Photobucket
The leading free image hosting website (MySpace-owned). Photobucket is extremely reliable and includes a very generous amount of bandwidth. Many free hosting services will cut off your images if too many people see them (uses up bandwidth), but it's very rare this would ever happen with Photobucket hosting. www.photobucket.com

Flickr
Another great image hosting website.
www.flickr.com

Slide
Image hosting with many slide show options. This is a
great site to get creative with your photos.
www.slide.com

ImageShack
Another widely used image hosting website, although
not as good as the first three.
www.imageshack.us

Free Video Hosting

MySpace TV
Good for hosting videos that correspond with a user's
MySpace profile to assist in gaining exposure. This
is especially important for bands, comedians, and
filmmakers. A MySpace video ties a video to a face
better than YouTube can. In many instances, both
services should be used.
www.myspacetv.com

YouTube
Great for hosting videos that need to be widely
available with the ability to be shared easily (also
known as viral videos).
www.youtube.com

Vixy
A free service that converts YouTube videos to
downloadable videos in several different formats.
http://vixy.net

Profile Components

Project Playlist
A popular, free music player for many different
networks including MySpace. It allows you to build
and update a playlist for your embedded music player
from endless choices of music.
www.projectplaylist.com

Sonific
Simple music player
www.sonific.com

Snocap
The official MySpace profile digital music player
and store. This flash-based music store can be placed
just about anywhere and has grown significantly in
2007. As of December 2007, unsigned artists pay a
commission fee of $0.39/download.
www.snocap.com

Gcast
Record podcasts (even over the phone) to play on your
MySpace profile.
www.gcast.com

SayNow
A voicemail box for your profile, allowing you or your users to record messages.
www.saynow.com

Snapvine
Another popular voicemail box, geared more towards the average user.
www.snapvine.com

Widgetbox
A great collection of widgets for your MySpace profile. Widgets are flash programs which could be games, news feeds, counters, clocks, slideshows, tools, and any other completely useful or useless, well, "widgets."
www.widgetbox.com

Profile Watcher
An excellent MySpace tracker, providing you with detailed, monthly graphs of your visitor information in real time.
www.myspacewatcher.com

Bots

Friend Blaster Pro
The only automation bot we now support given their longevity, customer support, consistent updates, and ease of use.
www.nickjag.com/friendblasterpro

Whore Trains

Google

Unfortunately, most whore train websites are usually deleted within a few months. Since this is the case, the easiest thing to do is to just search on the following queries in Google:

"whore train"

"k+"

"w4w"

"whore4whore"

"pc4pc"

"pic3pic"

Purchasing Friends, Bulletins, and Profiles

Digital Point
Marketplace for various services
http://forums.digitalpoint.com

MyspacePros
Marketplace for various services
www.myspacepros.com

Hit Generators

SoManyMp3s
Friend Requests and song plays increase
www.somanymp3s.com

Get Myspace Plays
Song plays increase
www.getmyspaceplays.com

Twenty-Four Hustle
Song plays increase
www.twentyfourhustle.com

Myspace Blogs and Forums

Mashable
Best social networking news website
www.mashable.com

MyspacePros
MySpace news, marketing, design, and marketplace
www.myspacepros.com

Grown Up Geek
News, trackers, and codes
http://grownupgeek.com/myspace-forum

Share your thoughts, techniques, and questions on the MySpace Marketing Forum, located on NickJag.com.

Special thanks to Jared Miller

www.ingramcontent.com/pod-product-compliance
Lightning Source LLC
Chambersburg PA
CBHW071225050326
40689CB00011B/2463